# In and Out the Windows

*Books by Ivy O. Eastwick*

# In and Out the Windows

happy poems for children
by

## Ivy O. Eastwick

set to music as
happy songs for children
by

## Marlys Swinger

illustrated by Gillian Barth

The Plough Publishing House, Rifton, New York

1971

*To Ada Campbell Rose*
*one-time Editor of*
*'Jack and Jill',*
*with love and gratitude*
*Ivy O. Eastwick*

First Printing 1969
Second Printing 1971

SBN 87486-007-5
Library of Congress Catalog Card Number 73-90841
Printed at the Plough Press, Farmington, Pa., U.S.A.

# Contents

The magical world of childhood—a world where clouds become woolly lambs and little horses and go racing across the sky, where little creatures take on the characteristics of children and do the things real children do—Ivy Eastwick has captured this world in these happy poems. Her Jenny and Johnnie who peep "in and out the windows" are like thousands of children everywhere who are filled with natural curiosity and joy.

Miss Eastwick's poems have been illustrated, set to music, and published at the Plough Publishing House by the Society of Brothers—communities where families and single people live together in a life of full sharing, based on the example of the early Christians. The Society makes its home in three places in the United States: Rifton, New York; Farmington, Pennsylvania; and Norfolk, Connecticut.

When the poems arrived at the Plough Publishing House, we all responded immediately to the happy world of childhood which Miss Eastwick described. The poems were read and re-read to our own children here; soon music appeared for twenty poems as Marlys Swinger felt their lively rhythm and wrote little tunes for them.

As for the illustrating of this book, it was natural for Gillian Barth to do it. Her own lively children appear again and again throughout the pages. She has added with her illustrations that touch of magic to combine the poems and music into a book you and your children will treasure and enjoy.

happy poems for children

# Jenny Looked Out of the Window

Jenny looked out of the window,
and what do you think she saw?
An old black rook,
a robin red,
a magpie and
a daw,
a blackbird in
the apple-tree
singing as loud
as any,
and a little dormouse
at the door of his house
looking back at Jenny.

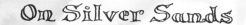

# On Silver Sands

Come for a run
by the silver sea,
come in the sunlight
with me, with me.
The sands are silver
beneath the sky—
more silver above them
the sea-birds fly.

Let us go running
away together
all in the spray-flying,
wind-sighing weather.

# Welcome, Spring

"Flyaway, Winter!
    Welcome, Spring!"—
these are the words
which the brown birds sing,
"Come with a primrose,
come with a lily,
violet,
candytuft,
daffydowndilly."

Flyaway, Winter!
Welcome, Spring,
bird-song,
flower-scent
and joy you bring.

4

# The Lovely Moments

A moment of sunshine,
a moment of shower,
a moment of apple-and-
cherry-tree-flower,
a moment of song,
and a moment of laughter—
that's April!    that's April!
with May coming after.

# The Dappled Fawn

The dappled fawn
gave a great big yawn,
he was tired
as a fawn
could be,
so he curled
in a heap
and he went
off to sleep
right under
the crab-apple tree,
and the shadow-and-dapple
of leaflet-and-apple,
they hid him away
from me.

# Watching Horses

The little white horse
runs very fast.
The little grey horse
runs faster.
But the little black horse
runs fastest of all—
he carries his little
young master.

# The Rose-Scented Geranium.

The Rose-scented Geranium
pretended to be a Rose—
    the Bee flew down,
    and buzzed around,
    deceived by his
    sensitive nose.

"The zzzzzzent," he buzzed,
"is the Rozzzzze'zzzzz   zzzzent,
I can zmell it upon the air,
but though my noze
sez it'z a Roze
my eyez,   my eyez declare
there iz no Roze anywhere!"

11

# I Can't See the Wind

I can't see the Wind,
but the Wind can see me—
it follows me, dancing,
across Lantern-lea,
it blows round my ankles,
it puffs through my hair,
it tangles me up till
I do not know where
or whither or thither
or why I'm this way,
the way of the Wind
on a merry March day.

# Jonathan's Kite

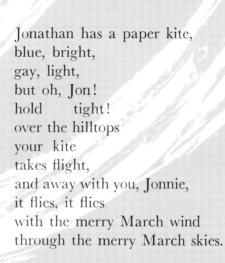

Jonathan has a paper kite,
very blue,
very bright,
with a raggedy tail
that goes flying away
with the merry March wind
on this merry March day.

Jonathan has a paper kite,
very gay,
very light,
and Jonathan watches it
rising high
to the uppermost part
of the merry March sky.

Jonathan has a paper kite,
blue, bright,
gay, light,
but oh, Jon!
hold        tight!
over the hilltops
your kite
takes flight,
and away with you, Jonnie,
it flies, it flies
with the merry March wind
through the merry March skies.

# And Here's a Pretty Thing!

Sing!
sing!
and here's a pretty thing—
a little lark carolling
up in the sky.
Sing!
sing!
and here's a pretty thing—
a woolly-cloud-lamb that is
galloping by.
Sing!
sing!
and here's a pretty thing—
a blackbird high up in
a russetty tree.
Sing!
sing!
and here's a pretty thing—
three children laughing
on Bilberry Lea.

15

# Is It Spring?

"Is it Spring?"
asked Little Bear
calling to his mother.

"Look out of the tree-trunk
and then you will see—
if the snow isn't snowing,
if the wind isn't blowing,
if the blossoms are budding
on the wild cherry-tree,
then it's SPRING!" said his mother,
"for you and for me."

# Somebody Said . . .

Somebody said:
"Spring"—
I do not know who.
In the green wood
a grey dove
was murmuring
"Cooooo,"
a squirrel
was chattering
high in an oak,
a jackdaw
was chuckling
at a mocking-bird's joke.

Somebody said:
"Spring" . . . .
a squirrel?
a bird?
or a child? . . .
I don't know,
but I know
what I heard—
I heard
the word:
"Spring."

# First Buttercups

Out of darkness,
out of earth,
Buttercups
with golden mirth
came up just
in time to see
Springtime run
across the lea;
and they could not
say for sure,
but they *thought*
that Springtime wore
a gay green gown
and golden shoes.........

Just the colors
THEY would choose!

# The Giraffe

The little Giraffe
was one foot tall—
scarcely bigger
than nothing-at-all,
and he wanted to touch
a star in the sky,
though he didn't know how
and he didn't know why;
so he stretched
and he stretched,
and he grew
and he grew
(in a way that no children
could possibly do)
and his neck
grew longer and longer and longer
while his wish
grew stronger

and stronger

and stronger.

At last he was quite
SIXTEEN  FEET  HIGH —

but he still couldn't reach

the star in the sky.

# Going to the Fair

The Bat
put on his leather hat,
the Cricket
in the clover
pulled on his summer socks
and shoes
and, last, his green
pullover;
then to the Fair
across the moor
the two friends went
together—
the Cricket
in his Lincoln-green,
the Bat
in his black leather.

# Little Grey Rabbit

The little Grey Rabbit
goes skippety-skip,
his grey tail behind him
goes flippety-flip,
he hears all around him
the merry birds sing
because it is Maytime
and Gaytime and Spring.

The little Grey Rabbit
goes hippety-hop,
his grey tail behind him
goes flippety-flop,
the lark in the blue sky,
the thrush in the tree
and little Grey Rabbit
are happy.   All three.

# Cherries and Cheese
## and Chocolate-Bars

Cherries
and cheese
and chocolate-bars—
do people
eat these
on the planet Mars?
Because,
if not,
I would rather stay
on Earth,
where they're eaten
every day.

# Apple-Pie

I simply do not know why I
should be so fond of apple-pie.

And when I'm offered it with cheese
*or* cream, I always say: "Yes, please."

And no one has to ask me twice—
I'll ALWAYS take a second slice.

## A Spade

A Spade's
a very useful thing
in Springtime for
the gardening;
in Wintertime
to dig the snow
and heap it in
a tidy row;
and when at last
the Summer's here
and skies are very
blue and clear,
and people pass
with nods and smiles,
and sandy beaches
stretch for miles,
and sea-birds call,
and sea-winds sing . . . . . .
a spade's
a very useful thing.

# The Foxglove

This Foxglove now
is taller than I—
it lifts its head
to the Midsummer sky,
and looks out over
the meadow and lea
to faraway boats
on the faraway sea.

30

# The Apple

This apple is ripe—
I watched it grow
after the melting
of winter-snow;
a pink flower bloomed
on its twisted tree
at last to flutter
away from me,
and a little green apple
appeared, right there,
in the glimmering,
shimmering,
summer air;
it looked at the sun,
and the sun smiled down
till the little green apple
turned golden-brown.

Now a sweet russet-apple
hangs on its tree,
nodding and smiling
at me.     At me.

31

# The Cloud

What caused the Cloud
to race over the hill?
The sun was warm
and the air was still
when the Cloud, shaped like
a little grey horse,
went rushing away
on a westward course.

I watched it gallop
along until
it vanished from sight
over Blueberry Hill.

## The Bookworm

While Mother sews
and scours and cooks
and cleans and scrubs,
I READ MY BOOKS.

# Coincidence

All on a winter's
morning-O
we took a walk
through the deep, steep snow;
we followed the track
of a rabbit grey
who had just been walking
along that way.

All on a summer's
morning-O,
through the singing woodlands
now we go;
and perhaps, perhaps
we shall see this way
the rabbit we trailed
on that winter's day.

# Winter-Walk

Rose-red
is the evening sky,
milk-white
is the snow,
let's go
on our evening-walk—
DO let us go.
Tomorrow the sky
may be dull and grey,
tomorrow the snow
may be gone,
so let us go
on a Winter's walk
in the last rays
of the sun.

# The Flyaway Birds

It's winter!
it's winter!
the birds are flying away
perhaps to the moon
where it's always June
and night's as bright as day.

When winter,
cold winter,
from the countryside has gone,
with flower and fern
will the birds return
with a song for everyone.

40

# A Happy Goodmorning

It is a happy morning—
there is blossom on the trees,
there's a merry robin singing,
there's a golden flight of bees,
there's a single dewdrop clinging
like a rainbow to a rose,
and the sun is busy shedding
little freckles on Jon's nose.

Oh, it IS a happy morning,
there is joy in everything,
such a good and happy morning
Jon has simply GOT to sing.

# The Moth

In the twilight
a green moth
encircles the room,
flying through
half-light,
through sunset-and-gloom;
if I see her
tomorrow
I know she will be
as silver
as sunlight
on the wild cherry-tree.

# Delphiniums and Nightingales

These blue delphiniums
in June
are nearly
as high as
the Midsummer Moon.

The songs of nightingales
in June
soar to
the sky and
the Midsummer Moon.

# Where ?

*Where does the Moon hide?*

Just behind the shadow
that's falling from
a bank of cloud
over Blackdown Meadow;
When the shadow
disappears—
as shadows always do—
the Moon will show
her silver face
again, to me and you.

## Deep in a Sea~Shell

Deep in a sea-shell
you will hear
the wind and the waves
and the moon, my dear.

The winds — they cry.
The waves — they sigh.
And the moon tells her secrets
to the wild sky.

# Johnnie Looked Out of the Window

Johnnie looked out of the window,
and what do you think he saw?
    A rabbit sitting
    there on the lawn,
    licking its little
    grey paw;
    it washed its face
    in morning-dew,
    it nibbled a sprig
    of clover,
    and then it raced
    to the garden-fence
and JUMPED RIGHT OVER!

happy songs for children

words by

Ivy O. Eastwick

music by

Marlys Swinger

# Jenny Looked Out of the Window

Jen-ny looked out of the win-dow, and what do you think she saw? An

old black rook, a rob-in red, a mag-pie and a daw, a

black-bird in the ap-ple-tree sing-ing as loud as an-y, and a

lit-tle dor-mouse at the door of his house look-ing back at Jen-ny.

# Johnnie Looked Out of the Window

John-nie looked out of the win-dow, and what do you think he saw? A

rab-bit sit - ting there on the lawn, lick-ing its lit-tle grey paw; it

washed its face in morn-ing-dew, it nib-bled a sprig of clo-ver, and

then it raced to the gar - den fence, and JUMPED RIGHT O-VER!

53

# A Happy Goodmorning

**Merrily**

It is a hap-py morn-ing—there is blos-som on the trees, ___ there's a
sin-gle dew-drop cling-ing like a rain-bow to a rose, ___ and the

mer-ry rob-in sing-ing, there's a gold-en flight of bees, there's a
sun is bus-y shed-ding lit-tle freck-les on Jon's nose. Oh, it

IS a hap-py morn-ing, there is joy in ev-'ry-thing, such a

good and hap-py morn-ing Jon has sim-ply GOT to sing. ___

# Welcome, Spring

**Brightly**

"Fly-a-way, Win-ter! Wel-come, Spring!"—these are the words which the

brown birds sing, "Come with a prim-rose, come with a li-ly,

vi-o-let, can-dy-tuft, daf-fy-down dil-ly." Fly-a-way, Win-ter!

Wel-come, Spring, bird-song, flower-scent and joy you bring.

# The Lovely Moments

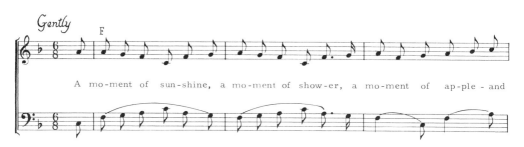

Gently

A mo-ment of sun-shine, a mo-ment of show-er, a mo-ment of ap-ple - and

cher-ry-tree-flow'r, a mo-ment of song, and a mo-ment of laugh-ter, that's

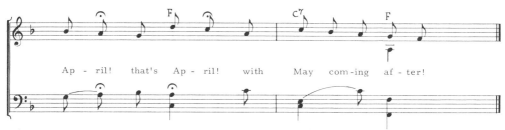

Ap - ril! that's Ap - ril! with May com-ing af - ter!

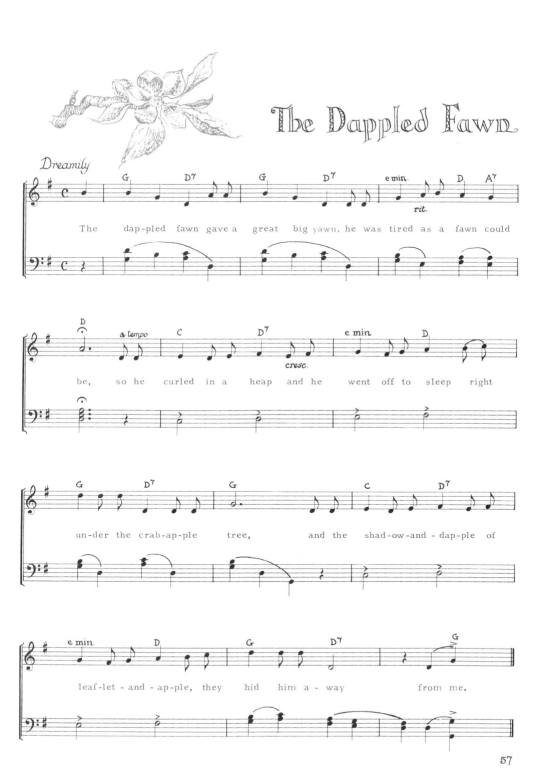

# The Dappled Fawn

Dreamily

The dap-pled fawn gave a great big yawn, he was tired as a fawn could

be, so he curled in a heap and he went off to sleep right

un-der the crab-ap-ple tree, and the shad-ow-and-dap-ple of

leaf-let-and-ap-ple, they hid him a-way from me.

# Watching Horses

*Gradually faster*

The lit-tle white horse runs ver - y fast. The lit-tle grey

horse runs fast - er. But the lit-tle black horse runs the

fast-est of all — he car-ries his lit-tle young mas - ter.

# I Can't See the Wind

*Swayingly*

I can't see the Wind, but the Wind can see me — it fol-lows me, danc-ing, a-

cross Lan-tern-lea, it blows round my ank-les, it puffs through my hair, it

tan-gles me up till I do not know where or whith-er or thith-er or

why I'm this way, the way of the Wind on a mer-ry March day.

# And Here's a Pretty Thing!

*With a gay lilt*

Sing! sing! and here's a pret-ty thing — a lit - tle lark car-ol-ling
Sing! sing! and here's a pret-ty thing — a black-bird high up in a

up in the sky. Sing! sing! and here's a pret-ty thing — a
rus-set-ty tree. Sing! sing! and here's a pret-ty thing—three

wool-ly - cloud - lamb that is gal - lop - ing by.
chil - dren laugh - ing on Bil - ber - ry Lea.

60

# First Buttercups

Whimsically

Out of dark-ness, out of earth, But-ter-cups with gold-en mirth
came up just in time to see Spring-time run a-cross the lea;
and they could not say for sure, but they thought that Spring-time wore a
gay green gown and gold-en shoes.... Just the col-ors THEY would choose!

# Going to the Fair

**Briskly**

The Bat put on his leath-er hat, the Crick-et in the clo-ver pulled
on his sum-mer socks and shoes and, last, his green pull - o - ver; then
to the Fair a-cross the moor the two friends went to-geth-er —— the
Crick-et in his Lin-coln-green, the Bat in his black leath-er.

# Little Grey Rabbit

Lightly

The lit-tle Grey Rab-bit goes skip-pe-ty-skip, his grey tail be-hind him goes
The lit-tle Grey Rab-bit goes hip-pe-ty-hop, his grey tail be-hind him goes

flip-pe-ty - flip, he hears all a - round him the mer-ry birds sing be-
flip-pe-ty - flop, the lark in the blue sky, the thrush in the tree and

cause it is May-time and Gay - time and Spring.
lit - tle Grey Rab-bit are hap - py. All three.

# Cherries and Cheese and Chocolate-Bars

*Wonderingly*

Cher-ries and cheese and choc'late-bars, cher-ries and cheese and choc'late-bars —do

peo-ple eat these on the plan-et Mars? Do peo-ple eat these on Mars? Be-

cause, if not, I'd rath-er stay, be - cause, if not, I'd rath-er stay on

Earth where they're eat-en ev-'ry day, on Earth where they're eat-en ev-'ry day.

Apple-Pie

Easily

I sim-ply do not know why I should be so fond of ap-ple-pie. I

ap-ple-pie. And when I'm of-fered it with cheese or

cream I al-ways say: "Yes, please." *(spoken)* And no one has to

ask me twice — I'll AL - WAYS take a se - cond slice.

A Spade

Cheerily

A Spade's a ver-y use-ful thing in Spring-time for the gar-den-ing; in
Win-ter-time to dig the snow and heap it in a

ti-dy-row; and when at last the Sum-mer's here and skies are ver-y blue and clear,

cresc.

and peo-ple pass with nods and smiles, and san-dy beach-es stretch for miles, and

sea-birds call, and sea-winds sing.. a spade's a ver-y use-ful thing.

66

# Coincidence

**Gaily**

All on a win-ter's morn-ing-O, morn-ing-O, morn-ing-O, we
All on a sum-mer's morn-ing-O, morn-ing-O, morn-ing-O, through the

took a walk through the deep, steep snow; deep, steep snow; we
sing-ing wood-lands now we go, now we go; and per-

fol-lowed the track of a rab-bit grey, rab-bit grey, rab-bit grey, who had
haps, per-haps we shall see this way, see this way, see this way the

just been walk-ing a-long that way, a-long that way.
rab-bit we trailed on that win-ter's day, that win-ter's day.

67

# Winter-Walk

Peacefully

Rose-red is the eve-ning sky, milk-white is the snow,

let's go on our eve-ning-walk — do, do let us go. To-

mor-row the sky may be dull and grey, to-mor-row the snow may be gone, so

let us go on a Win-ter's walk in the last rays of the sun.

# The Moth

*Delicately*

In the twi-light a green moth en - cir - cles the room,
fly - ing through half-light, through sun-set - and - gloom; if I
see her to - mor - row I know she will be as
sil - ver as sun - light on the wild cher - ry - tree.

# On Silver Sands

**Smoothly**

Come for a run by the sil-ver sea, come in the sun-light with

me, with me. The sands are sil-ver be-neath the sky — more

sil-ver a-bove them the sea-birds fly. Let us go run-ning a-

way to-geth-er all in the spray-fly-ing, wind-sigh-ing weath-er.

# Deep in a Sea-Shell

**Thoughtfully**

Deep in a sea-shell you will hear the wind and the waves and the

moon, my dear. The winds — they cry. The waves — they sigh. And the

moon tells her se - crets to the wild sky.